"The Great Ideas Process gave the companies I work with results and changed how I see opportunities. At Stewart and Stevenson, it gave us a way to increase our revenues by $425 million in four months."

-- Jay Manning, *President and CEO of Equisales, former VP of Stewart & Stevenson, GM Global Sales of General Electric*

"Your success in turning around a difficult management challenge in a short time period greatly exceeded our expectations. You and your team have a good grasp of our people issues and our business. We found the teaching methodology you utilized especially effective. Your approach to the planning process was very effective. It was surprising to us how well you were able to help the group focus on the key issues and reach a consensus."

-- Barry M. Granger, *Vice President, DuPont Government Marketing and Government Affairs*

"Jackie, You were just fabulous!!! Thanks so much for agreeing to speak with just a few weeks notice. Many of the women I spoke to after just raved about you and said that you brought up critical energy infrastructure issues that we haven't heard addressed before. Your speaking style is so warm, friendly, engaging, as well as extremely knowledgeable."

-- Karyl M. Lawson White,
Founder, Women's Energy Network

"Great Ideas has inspired our organization to think in ways we would not have realized without it. We have discovered the language that opens up an array of business and industry partnerships among people and companies that share our vision and work toward healthier communities!" These principles make even good people better!"

-- Steven R. Shelton, *M.B.A, PA-C, Assistant Vice President for Community Outreach and Program Director, UTMB-Health, Texas Area Health Education Center, East*

"You did an excellent job, clearly meeting and exceeding my expectations. Our morale, effectiveness, and determination have already improved noticeably as a result of the retreat. I am so glad we made the decision to benefit from your talents."

-- Richard A. Huebner,
Executive Director, Houston Minority Supplier Development Council, Inc.

"Jackie, I must complement you and your team on a very effective training process. The training was very practical and well executed. Based on the comments received from the attendees, it was the most effective training seminar any of them had ever attended."

-- J. M. Hofmann, *Executive VP, K.M.M. Holdings, Inc.*

"Jackie Broussard is an accomplished master at helping you take your company to the next level and beyond."

-- Jeff Share, *Editor, Pipeline & Gas Journal*

Transformational
Growth

This book is dedicated to you.

I am grateful to Jules. Your love and strength encourage me. My writing and creativity are supported with love from my family and friends including the boys, John and Bob, Mom and Joe Jackson, Judy Sheffield, Sydney Sheffield, Reagan Sheffield, Betty Hubenthal, Margaret Weed Greenshield, Elinor Hart, Susan Lynn, Robyn Drake, Jessica Trapp, Devan Tindall, Deedie Root, Ph.D., Gigi, Hubert, and Brunette.

I am so grateful for the continued persistence, enthusiasm, and advocacy of Suzy Ginsburg with your creative team and Mickey Barbely. Thank you for being so incredibly talented and kind.

Transformational Growth has evolved with the brilliance of our specialists, clients, partners, mentors, friends, and supporters. With your love, compassion, and willingness, transformational growth is happening in the world.

TRANSFORMATIONAL GROWTH

GREAT IDEAS PROCESS™

JACKIE BROUSSARD

MATHEWS DUNCAN

_____

TEXAS

ISBN-13:978-0615492476

Written by Jackie Broussard
Great Ideas Process™
Great Ideas Company
Houston, Texas
www.greatideasco.com

713.520.9600
jackie@greatideasco.com

Printed and bound In The United States of America

Table of Contents

I. Introduction

The revolutionary "Great Ideas Process™" helps organizations secure innovative and creative partnerships that ensure future growth, inspire positive change, and create lasting connections to transform their organization, business, and community.

Sparking Connections!

The Great Ideas Process™ gives leaders the necessary tools to build new strategic partnerships that support opportunities for expansion. To ensure sustainable, long-term success, this process goes beyond the typical networking program and business interactions and emphasizes entrepreneurial growth tactics to enhance the future of your organization. Through a continued focus on the ever-changing market, industry trends by segment, and more opportunities to expand, we help you build global collaborations that mean peace and profitability for your organization. Providing the framework, the Great Ideas Process™ gives leaders the ability to quickly build a cost-efficient strategy for growth and transformation.

1. Great Ideas Summit™: This open, creative, discovery forum enables your current or potential supporters to gather in a roundtable-based setting to plan a course of action and define what types of opportunities they see in the future for a larger vision, such as Making Our Communities Healthier. These current or potential supporters and the organization will collaborate to accomplish growth, expand their business practices, and learn more about what the community wants and needs. The summit provides the foundation for implementing your organizational expansion, leadership development, and business strategies.

2. Action Plan: With your vision and business goals in mind, the Great Ideas Action Plan allows you to organize and implement measurable steps to spark achievable solutions. This plan is a course of action that will be applied to your overall progress and drive funding support opportunities. The action plan allows for a 90-day period to achieve visible and sustainable personal and professional growth.

3. Partnerships: By driving funding support and increasing strategic workflow, the connections provided through partner relationships are key factors for exponential growth. Along with these partnerships, certain initiatives are begun in order to build an effective long-term plan. With each connection made, opportunities emerge to support sustainable increases of your targeted goals. Within a developing partnership comes research on new trends in each industry. As such trends lead to new ventures, special training sessions or conferences are held to capture the essentials of these developments, such as our session on "Internal and External Partnering."

Willing and Able.

Are you willing and able to change? Some people and organizations are not willing to change and/or are not able to because they believe the timing is not right for change. Some think they are too near retirement to rock the boat; some have been in a job for 30 years and see only one way to do it; others are too burned-out to change. Some organizations are so invested in the status quo or the fight for survival that they don't have time to change until they are forced to by their funding sources, such as when the federal or state governments make budget cuts.

Partners and leaders who are unwilling and unable to change are not good candidates for the Great Ideas Process™. It is important to determine if the leaders in your organization are willing and able to take baby steps to start to change. If they are not, one-on-one planning with these individuals to find what can be done for them – perhaps training or individual mentoring to find a way to initiate change – is vital if they are going to be partners or leaders in the future plans for the organization.

Resistance from leaders and partners can take tremendous energy, time, and funding. After 60 days in the process with one of our clients, we worked with the Vice President of the division to identify the divisional budget and plan. In tracking the progress, four leaders excelled in activity, attitude, and performance, while four others complained, had little activity, and made excuses for not performing. The Vice President decided to invest in the four leaders who were excelling. The change was remarkable. With additional training and support involving partners, the four leaders excelled and doubled the historic growth rate of the organization in 18 months. The four leaders who were underperforming were aided in transitioning elsewhere. This early decision freed up more resources and time by assisting two to retire and two to find their passion in other divisions.

Working with willing and able leaders and partners ready to apply the four basic principles of the Great Ideas Process™ will make a tremendous difference in lowering the cost of implementing change. The principles of the Great Ideas Process™ are:

1. Focus on What You Can Do for Others. Put the communities and clients you work with at the center of your thoughts, plans, and actions. In all you do, work *with* people and not *for* them. This focus has improved our results dramatically, and we have seen the same thing happen with clients.

2. **Laugh Out Loud**. Take action with others to build trust and experience laughter. Enjoy the journey. It is an amazing insight when we learn something new and take the pressure off others and ourselves.

3. Tighten Up. Back in the 60s Archie Bell and the Drells from Henderson, Texas, had the number one hit, "Tighten Up." Archie had a way of making stale things fresh. "Tighten Up" refers to immediate focus, which introduces a new vitality or life force into relationships. The more specific we become, the better and faster results flow.

4. Agree On Where to Start and Take Action with Partners. How much more efficient could we be if we gave up wasting time on resistance? What if we ignore our critics and make progress with our supporters? Trying to get people to work with us, like us, be supportive, is exhausting. What is possible if we spend our time working with key strategic leaders who can influence at least 1,000 people and make substantial change in the lives of millions? Aligning our goals with strategic partners and building strong relationships to support and share our success benefits our communities and clients as well as ourselves.

II. Great Ideas Summit™

The Great Ideas Summit™ is a creative, highly interactive forum for partnering with community and business leaders to agree on a starting point for a new change initiative, such as "Making Our Communities Healthier." It gives the organization, community, and business leaders a fresh approach and new direction to change the status quo for addressing old problems.

When selecting internal leaders as well as current and potential supporters for summit participation, it is important that each participating leader wants to learn how to:

❖ See options beyond the status quo.

❖ Be open to partner in different ways.

❖ Say "Yes" to change and doing something for the first time.

The Great Ideas Process™ is a spiral model of Action Planning, which keeps repeating and going up to another level of performance as organizations continue to change, learn, and grow. The

Great Ideas Summit™ is one part of the process that can be completed in a linear, step-by-step fashion to help leaders consider the necessary ingredients to make change faster, less costly, and easier for the people in the organization and the community.

While there are tools such as checklist and setup des-criptions listed as supplemental materials, the basic steps are:

Step One – Put the Community at the Center.

"When you drew the circle with the community in the center, I got it. I know why we are making this change. We are not struggling to survive anymore and waiting to see what we get from the government. We are thriving.

We are focusing on the people, business leaders, who want what we want; A better, healthier community." – *Tom Knight, Director, East Texas AHEC North Central Operations.*

When putting the community at the center, one useful tool is to visualize one person you know benefitting from change in the status quo. This humanizes the change within the community. Putting the community at the center inspires the leaders and organization to leave old problems behind. It gives people permission to be right instead of being wrong. This new focus rallies energy and begins to heal the organization. It usually encourages people to take on a cause and perform at a higher level. It has a growing effect for the organization. It creates more peace and less anger in the organization.

Step Two – Define What Kind of Partners Want What You Want.

"What we want is the connection to business and industry leaders." – *Steven R. Shelton, MBA, PA-C, Executive Director, East Texas Area Health Education Center (AHEC)*

Steve is right. It is the connection to business and global industry leaders that puts health organizations on a sustainable track. Businesses think in terms of economic value or money. They look at what health care costs, in terms of the costs of doing business in a community today and into the future. Considering the connection to economic value for the potential partners who drive prosperity forward is vital to the sustainability of an organization that makes communities healthier. It opens new levels on competency and vision for the future of the communities to improve the overall community health. Adding physical health to economic health provides a very profitable outcome for people, businesses, industries, organizations, and communities.

Step Two to the Great Ideas Process™ is to define what kind of partners want what you want and measure the value.

We do this with a Value Model I designed in collaboration with V. Kumar, Ph.D. V. Kumar is an international marketing expert and author of many marketing research books, including *International Marketing Research*. He helped us design our initial value model, and mentored us in working with an academic medicine client to look at the perception of value in a double competency model.

The first level of competency used secondary research in current published data about the results and outcome of value perceptions in a community or service delivery category. This included examining the positive value that will be created from the outcome that collaborative partners want the community to achieve. For example, one health collaboration wants their community to be ranked as the most peaceful community in the state by a credible third party. Robert Wood Johnson Foundation's University of Wisconsin study is the credible third party, which tracks health factors for all counties in each state and the United States. By focusing on nationally published data and taking collaborative positive actions, it is possible for counties to improve their health factors.

The second level of competency is interviews or research with industry and business leaders. This primary research is completed in three phases:

1. Asking the organizational leaders to agree on their answers to questions that establish the scope and

direction of the work. The questions are:

❖ What is the big issue they want to join with the community to solve?

❖ How do they want to see their organization a year from now?

❖ What are the qualities of the potential partners who will help achieve that goal in one year?

❖ What motivates these leaders?

❖ What benefits would partners bring to them?

❖ What values do the partners have in common?

2. Defining groups of people or industry segments who fit the qualities and are connected to receive value or benefits from the outcome of the collaboration. For example, the largest employer in a community would benefit from a community health network.

3. Researching the connected key leaders with the same values in each of the segments of people or organizations and deter-

mining the scope of the assignment – for example, within the utility's defined service area for CenterPoint Energy or the world for GE. Another example is grocery stores, where HEB is a leader in the segment and very connected to other leaders.

Step Three – Get Curious and Ask Questions.

A Great Ideas Specialist, Jim Norman, once referred to the process of asking the right questions as "Jackie Magic." To me that was funny, because anyone can have that kind of magic. It's a type of magic that belongs to every one of us, no matter who we are or where we came from. And, just as important, it's a type of magic that we can all use to benefit ourselves as well as those around us.

Questions are at the heart of great ideas. And they are, in fact, magical in a variety of ways.

First, good questions establish credibility. This is the core of advice that drives change. This is what makes an idea great. It comes from a person we believe in and who offers credibility, integrity and substance. It is the magic bullet of growth.

What are good questions?

I realized this when I was driving in a freezing storm from Pennsylvania to Ohio. At the time, I was riding in a Ford Taurus with Neal, a client with a large manufacturing company. As we carefully made our way through the elements, Neal suddenly asked me what made the difference between everyday questions and good questions. I said it involved a number of factors, including the questions themselves, the order, and the timing. He was amused and asked me for more details. Since we had nowhere to go but along a freezing Interstate, I shared my thoughts.

❖ *Don't be too personal at first.*

Most of us have a desire to connect with people, to help each other. We want to interact with another human. But when you ask a question, start with one that's specific but not particularly personal. Examples: "What are your responsibilities?" "What are your priorities?"

The reason these are good starting questions is that they are particular in their focus, but comfortable enough for most people. We have asked these questions in more than 1,000 conversations with business, community, and health care leaders. We found the vast majority could answer these questions immediately with extreme confidence. It makes sense: we all have responsibilities and priorities, so why be shy talking about them?

The best way to ask the questions depends on the results you want. In-person questions can be the most powerful and time-consuming. By contrast, a question on the phone can reveal many more intricate details that many people are not comfortable discussing face-to-face. Whatever venue you choose, don't deliver questions via writing or email. It depersonalizes the approach.

❖ *Examine individual situations.*

Now we can move on to the next question in the sequence, which deals with specifics for a business, organization, or community. One great question we have tested with our clients, their potential customers, and community leaders is, "What is your greatest challenge right now?"

This encourages the person to examine their current situation and, from there, discuss where their attention, resources, time, and energy are focused. This provides immediate clues – an opportunity to connect, solve, or lend assistance that can make a difference with that person. On some assignments, we ask a few more questions about the future, including: "What is on the horizon for your industry? Organization? Community?"

With our manufacturing clients, this was vital because the industry is constantly changing. At one point, the industry was facing changes in regulations and, as a result, change came in the form of retirements (we attended more than three retirement parties in a month!).

❖ *On to the future together!*

The third question in the sequence works to bring you together sometime in the future with the person to whom you're talking. For instance: "Imagine a year from now. You have met the challenges you identified. What would it look like to you?" This opens up some creativity. The person answering the question may start to laugh, but it's surprising how often they come up with some amazingly simple, yet powerful, views of the future.

Those can lead the way to significant breakthroughs – in both planning and execution.

❖ *Identify value.*

The fourth question is usually about value, such as "What value would you derive from this idea?" This can really open new ideas because it hits at the heart of many issues – what the person answering the question stands to gain.

What's also interesting about this particular question is that it can elicit ideas that many people have considered but never shared with anyone else – the stereotypic "I thought about this a lot but have never actually talked about it with anyone else." This is another potential breakthrough point. Moreover, it also changes the dynamics between the person asking the questions and the person answering them – creating a sense of connection and trust.

❖ *How can we stay in touch?*

The fifth question is about how to communicate the idea and work together to help it grow. It is usually: "What is the best way to contact you with a new idea?" This tells you precisely how someone wants to stay in touch and gives you immediate access to communicating in that fashion. It opens the door for continued discussions.

By the way, the sequence of the questions is very important! We had a credibility psychologist help us with the questioning sequence and model design. When you ask a question that is well-written, well-timed, and in the right order, people give careful consideration to their answers and do their best to answer them. That means better information and better communication.

Now that we've covered the sorts of questions you can ask and in what order, let's take a closer look at what actually transpires during the process.

How do you ask good questions?

❖ *Good questions asked in the right order establish credibility.*

How do questions establish credibility? They show a thoughtful consideration and interest in the other person. They show you are willing to let it be the other person's idea. You are willing not to take all the credit. You are willing to be open, to listen, and to be caring. You do not want to foist your opinion, push advice, or sell something. You believe the person is so valuable that you will write their answers down and take action on them. What gives the questions credibility to the person asking and the group or organization that person represents is that they care enough to find out what is important to the other person – and, from there, genuinely value that person's ideas.

A client, Keith Marple of CenterPoint Energy in Oklahoma, said, "These questions are amazing to me. I had no idea the friend I sat next to each week for lunch was making a major equipment change in his hospital, which dramatically changed the load of natural gas he used. When we went to his office and asked the questions, my eyes were opened by the decisions he had made in the last year. It gave me a whole new way to see him and our relationship. The client sees us in a different way. We are now invited to his statewide industry meetings to present our latest technologies."

❖ *Good questions align the organization, partners, and communities for results.*

When you direct the right question to the right person at the right time, you not only gain instant credibility with them, you reposition yourself. Put another way: when you ask the right questions at the right time, you're not the center of attention, the hub of the universe. Rather, it puts you alongside the person as a collaborator, a partner, and a true supporter.

Those with whom you partner will provide funding, revenue, clients, support, encouragement, referrals, members, and new opportunities.

❖ *Have someone else start the process.*

How can we be sure we're approaching the right person with the right question at the right time? Think back to seventh grade in school. We all remember asking a trusted friend whether a certain boy or girl liked us. We didn't know it at the time, but we were tuning into an essential dynamic to gain access to the truth. People who succeed in launching new initiatives or seeing a project through to eventual success often have someone else ask important questions for them to make sure they have the right approach and a receptive audience. To refer to it in schoolyard terms, if you want to dance, make sure the person you ask is going to say yes.

It's vital to get someone else to ask first so you have the right approach. Moreover, there's tremendous value and support with a third party asking questions on your behalf.

You will get a completely fresh perspective. They will hear, see, and find out completely new information from what you yourself will. The next time the ideal customer or community leader is contacted, you can ask the questions. You will hear something completely different.

One of our clients, a woman-owned company, has been recognized as one of Houston's 100 fastest growing companies. This focused company places IT professionals in the energy sector, and the company's ideal client was a chief information and technology executive of very large multinationals. To find out what our client needed to know, we acted as the third party to ask questions. What we found is the executives wanted our client to specialize in an area so that our client could guarantee the best talent in the right specialty. Our client made the change and is

on the fastest growing list
again. The company's
leadership said the four months
we worked with them and
asked questions for them was
one of the most personally and
professionally rewarding
experiences they've ever had.

Who's the ideal third party? It
needs to be someone who, if
you will, is disinterested but
engaged. They are not
necessarily doing this to get a
job or support a cause or a
person. The ideal third party is
open-minded, creative, a good
listener, does not take sides,
and makes everyone feel
accepted, valued, and
appreciated. It can be almost

anyone who is trained in the Great Ideas Process™ and is an active listener – a leader in education, professional development, business person, volunteer, an adviser, a retired person, or a friend, just so long as it's someone who knows how to let the other person talk, listens well, and have his or her say.

Tom Pace, Senior Pastor at St. Luke's United Methodist Church, in a letter to me, wrote: "We just wanted to thank you for the work you have done with the Gethsemane and St. Luke's Partnership. You have been invaluable in a number of ways. First, you provided the impetus to keep this project moving forward; without you, it may have very well stalled along the way. Your persistence paid off and kept us on track. Second, you have provided a neutral party to help each of us feel we had a voice in the process. Finally, you really did help to expand our vision, to make it something bigger than we are. You did that by introducing us to so many amazing people and relationships that will pay off dramatically as we move into implementation."

So, give some thought to using a third person to, in effect, start the process of asking the right questions, posed in the right order to the right person. An outside person can make all the difference, as we've seen in our work with companies and groups that tried to do all this internally. They were well-intentioned, but all of their efforts were managed, processed, and interpreted by internal people, who were limited in their approach by their own preconceptions. The information they developed was just a filtered version of the existing culture and a confirmation of their own thinking.

Back to the story that started this chapter. At the time, Neal was evaluating us for a roll out of a new sales approach for a manufacturing company. It was between Great Ideas Process™ and a sales training company. After hearing my explanation about what makes a good question, he said we were much more than just sales training, just as a great question is so much more than an average one. It was like comparing a Lamborghini with a Ford Taurus. Both will get you there. One is just with more style, faster, and a lot more fun. Both will take you from point "A" to point "B." It is how you want to go and the substance and quality of the movement. It's all about great questions.

Step Four – Learn to Collaborate with Focus.

The most effective collaboration focuses on a very specific, short time frame for a specific approach for a specific opportunity. This is the approach we take with Great Ideas Process, a creative, interactive forum to solve One Big Issue with partners.

The Great Ideas Process™ gives current or potential supporters the freedom to not know all the answers, have the solution, or solve something alone. It is a supportive learning environment in which everyone is free to work together, to gather in a forum-based setting to analyze the answers to questions in Step Three from potential partners in Step Two.

In this session, agreement happens through a new approach – working together. This approach is for a non-traditional course of action aimed at specific types of opportunities participants see in the future for a larger vision, such as Making Our Communities Healthier. The current or potential supporters and the organization will accomplish growth, expand their business practices, and learn more about what the community wants and needs. The Great Ideas Summit™ provides the foundation for implementing organizational expansion, leadership development, and business strategies.

To prepare for the Great Ideas Summit™, the key leader will analyze the responses to the questions into three categories: challenges, opportunities, and immediate action. Results will be shared in a presentation, usually in PowerPoint, video, or with posters.

The key leaders and their supporters will call, email, mail, and invite 60 or so leaders with whom they completed interviews and ask current supporters, as well as staff and board members to attend, with the intention of hosting a Great Ideas Summit™ with 30 attendees.

* ❖ ***Where you have it matters.***

We have found if you have a venue that is interesting, such as Rice's Cohen Faculty Club, people will want to come. Leaders are interested to see what they can learn and how they can solve an issue with the other partners attending. It helps tremendously if you have a welcoming speaker and well-known attendee. One Vice President of a large development company who experienced such a meeting said, "Rarely do I ever get to think creatively and enjoy learning. Today was a very good day for me. Thank you."

❖ *Give people a chance to amaze you.*

Listen to the guest you invited. We recommend a highly interactive session where the presentation is usually 10 minutes and facilitated exponential interaction is 80 minutes, with 20 minutes of breaks, and working lunch. It is vital for the staff and board to meet and greet everyone to make them feel at home in the environment and appreciated.

❖ *Ask what value solving this big issue creates for the participants.*

Open the summit by asking each person to speak for 30 seconds or so to describe the value that solving this big issue, "Making Our Communities Healthier," creates for them. You will be astonished at what you hear. To hear John, manager of large retail organization in Austin, say, "I spend millions a year on health benefits for my employees and we need help for a healthier community" brings relevance to Making Our Communities Healthier from his perspective.

❖ *Talk of immediate action flames enthusiasm.*

In the next part of the Great Ideas Summit™, the Great Ideas Certified facilitator asks each person to give his or her 30-second perspective on immediate action that can be taken for "Making Our Communities Healthier." This creates an exponential effect. Each leader around the room is sitting in a horseshoe-shaped arrangement and is considering what pithy point they want to make. It makes it fun and energizing.

> ❖ *Present the opportunities from the conversations of 20 potential partners.*

In 11 minutes or less, the analysis of the conversations opens new discussion points for the community connections you are now forming. The partners are starting to come together to see themselves as participants in this process. One very effective way to do the presentation is to invite three of the leaders to present each of the slides in the PowerPoint show or video clips, and for them to give a 30-second narrative on what it means to them. This builds more credibility for the relevance for the data. The facilitator invites each person to take a piece of colored paper and a marker. The facilitator lets the participants know this is a timed exercise for two minutes, and invites them to draw an image of how they see this partnership working a year from now when they are together making our communities healthier – the particular big issue we want to address. People giggle and do it. It is amazing the quality of conceptual drawings we have seen. At this point, the facilitator directs the hosting team to serve the working lunch. As people are finishing up lunch, the facilitator tapes the drawings up around the room. Each person is asked to take a marker and put a check by the drawing that best tells the story of how they see the results of the big issue a year from now. The facilitator takes the drawing with the most checks and posts it to the middle of the flip chart.

❖ *Develop the key opportunities.*

To spur more creativity, the facilitator asks each person who did not present to speak for 30 seconds about what they think the organization and this partnership could do better, differently, or for the first time, reflecting the key opportunities we began to develop in the conversations. Each participant is invited to take about 20 pieces of paper and a marker. In a two-minute, timed exercise with Mozart or Vivaldi classical upbeat music, the facilitator invites the participant to write one idea per page, starting with an action word and using three to seven words per page to answer the question, "What would you do differently, better, or for the first time to achieve this image so we are making our communities healthier?" The participants take a break.

The facilitator and assistants tape the ideas on the wall. The next step is for the Action Planning to begin.

III. Action Plan

At 1:00 PM, in most Great Ideas Summits, Action Planning begins. Some clients want to start with the Action Plan instead of the Great Ideas Summit™, and this works also. We have a particular collaboration that has been very successful for two years in working the action plan, collectively created by the participants. The benefit of the Great Ideas Summit™ is sustainability, momentum building, and rapidly connecting more than 20 potential partners at one time. It gives a much richer, fully textured, and thoughtful Action Plan with a very wide array group of planners at the Great Ideas Summit™, such as corporate executives, physicians, administrators, energy companies, nonprofits, entrepreneurs, government agencies, law enforcement, manufacturing, staff members, local foundations, and national foundations. More partners provide stronger plans working together. The purpose of the first 20 minutes session is to build a framework and for each person to decide what interest them individually. This is the hardest point for many people, but the results can be tremendous. After one pipeline services client decided where to start and continued with the plan, the company increased its revenues by $100 million in six months. By starting the Action Plan, momentum builds and organizational change occurs. With a Great Ideas Summit™ to build the infrastructure for the change and add depth and specificity to the research, change has relevance and comes from outside of the organization. Staff and board members start to introduce change into the organization after reading the specific interviews with potential partners. The relevance and awareness of the value of what the organization is creating with the community and partners gives roots to the work. It is grounded and relevant to what is happening around them. The community and partners will nurture the organization to succeed at never-before-imagined levels. It will take the limits and silos out of the community to better serve the clients or customers. The partners, staff, board members, and clients will find a way for the organization to thrive. It builds support and relevance for the success of the community and surrounding businesses.

Go With What Interest You.

Now, back to the partners and participants that convened at the Great Ideas Summit™. Each of the ideas is grouped into categories by the participants, who develop a name for each category. Usually, the participants are asked to stand and move around the room. This is very helpful after lunch to keep the energy flowing. The focus on this Action Planning task is to decide which category of connected Action Items will start the success of 80 percent of the results.

The participants remove the Action Item papers from the walls and put them into piles with the category name on the top. The stacks of paper are bound together and each stack is turned face down.

Categories are named, and this is framework for the Action Plan.

Who Works on What?

The Action Items from the category are placed on tables around the room or on one long table. The items are face up. The participants can hold the items in front of them when they find one item that interests them. The participants look and see if any of the other items go together and are to be combined. Participants decide how quickly each item will be done and who will work on it. This usually takes about two hours, depending on the organization. Then, the Action Plan is written with an Executive Summary and both are presented to potential partners for their support.

Great Ideas Internal and External Partnering Training to Help to Complete the Details of the Plan.

With many organizations, we find Great Ideas Training and Support is invited in work with staff members, board members, and volunteers to complete an Action Plan. With this Training and Support, and Action Planning assistance, the individuals or smaller teams begin to work out the details of the plan and complete their action items. With Great Ideas Training and Support for Making Our Communities Healthier, Janis Ritter and Jill Clements, Executive Directors of East Texas AHEC Regional Operations are leading the way. They have made excellent progress and are attracting the support of more business leaders, foundation leaders willing to advocate with other foundations on their behalf, and volunteers willing to donate time and money to the cause.

IV. Partnerships

Most of our clients want to find ways to work with their internal and external partners. Many clients see internal supporters, volunteers, funders, clients, patients, physicians, and customers as partners. This is not something many have extensive success or training to do in this new "interdisciplinary or cross cultural teams." When we started to work with East Texas AHEC's Director of Rural & Regional Programs, Mary Wainwright said, "We have over 3,000 partners. Traditionally, we go to them when we have federal or state grant funding and ask them to join us. They rarely ask us to join them in funding or pay us for our services. They look to us to provide services for free. We want to transform these partnerships to more supporting partners and businesses." Mary is very clear on what she wants from partnerships.

The Great Ideas Process™ begins with putting the local community, including the patients and customers, at the center. Do you and your partner share this value? If the answer is yes, then ask questions we discussed in the

Great Ideas Summit™. When you hear your partner's answers to your questions, do you see a fit for your organization in their future? If the answer is yes, then communicating where you see the benefit for the partner and what you from the partnership is important. If the partner says yes and agrees, asking if you can present the options to them for investing in the partnership is important.

Great Ideas Internal and External Partnering, Planning, and Leading Courses.

The ability to build solid partnerships is a key element to the sustainability of organizations. Focusing on being relevant to the local community and on supporters' desire for economic efficiency makes sense for organizations serving the same clients. There is an efficiency and focus for finding new ways to work together to lower costs and improve the quality of the work. Partnerships have a short-term value and a long-term value. When organizations start to look at the long-term value of a partner, they begin to become clear on how important it is to nurture the relationships.

The Great Ideas Process™ offers supporting internal and external partnering.

It also provides leadership development. The planning and leading courses are customized to each client's particular vision, culture, situation, and action plan in ways that benefit their own clients and volunteers or partners. These customized professional development training sessions focus on how to ask questions, present options, and gain agreement for levels of support to accomplish the shared vision for the organization. In many of the planning and leading courses, we calculate the economic lifetime value of a partnership, which can be encouraging from each of the partners' perspectives. With a large energy client, we calculated the economic lifetime value of a partnership with a customer and developer to install natural gas into a multifamily project. The calculation reflected three viewpoints – the tenant customer's, our client's, and the developer's. Everyone could see the value, and it increased the customer count by 55,000 for our client in 18 months. It also increased the value of the properties for developers by changing the rent rate and lowered the utility costs for the tenant. Everyone could see the value.

The Economic Lifetime Value of a Partnership.

The economic lifetime value of the relationship can be calculated and analyzed for each organization. It creates a network, with each calculation connected to many others. Many people know each other, and if it you make it easy and safe for them, they will connect you to others. When you connect to an industry leader, you connect to at least 300 more contacts. When MetLife researched the top agents, they found that, while most knew 100 people, top performers knew 300, and the 300 they knew were connected to thousands more. The business and industry leaders we research are connected to where the economic development or financial strength is pooling in a local community.

Economic Value Builds Speed in Collaboration.

When we interviewed Economic Development Directors, many struggled with connecting the value of the economic future of a community to the health of its citizens. This is an easy connection for Leslie Hargrove, Executive Director, East Texas AHEC Coastal Regional Operations. In Matagorda County, she identified the economic value of one primary care physician to be $1.8 million to the local economy. Each physician creates four jobs and becomes a role model for local students to aspire to continue their education. Imagine the avoided costs for employers if employees have local health care services.

In the current economy, many employees will avoid health

care visits they fear will identify them as a business liability.

Janice Ford Griffin, National Program Director of Robert Wood Johnson Foundation's Community Health Leaders, speaks of her work in local communities, where businesses and school nurses were interviewed. The school nurses were being asked for health advice and care by insured and employed parents who did not want their employer to know about their condition. The Human Resource Departments manage the health care and are involved in employment decisions for employees. There is an interconnectedness of health for the employed and insured as well as the unemployed and uninsured that is overlooked in many traditional community health initiatives.

When clients participate in training with the Great Ideas Process™, it is personalized to their immediate situation. When clients want to change the way they do business, our training supports the revolutionary part of the process.

Because learning to do things better can be revolutionary, we design our training to work by engaging all of the learner's senses. Jay Manning, President and CEO of Equisales, former VP of Stewart & Stevenson, GM Global Sales of General Electric, in our first meeting said, "I want some action, not just a binder." We agree. This is our mantra. Our training is effective because it is designed with the learner and their local community at the center, surrounded by partners with the same values and goals. Leaders want a simple formula and proven tools to take action.

V. Partners and Transformation

After client leaders and their partners agree on shared values and the way they will use values in every day work to inspire completing an action plan, the transformation can begin. The more committed and effective the partnership is, the greater the transformation can be.

Consider East Texas AHEC and its community health mission. Walmart, with its 4,000 US stores, hundreds of thousands of employees and millions of shoppers, is large enough to be a transformational partner that sparks change. When change starts to happen, then real growth will occur. Walmart knows this, because that is how it has become a leader. It has for years partnered and worked with suppliers to achieve the lowest cost in the United States. Walmart's efforts alone would not be enough to win long-term sustainable growth and customer loyalty.

What we have learned in the Great Ideas Process™ is that for organizations to transform, the change they seek must matter to someone outside of the organization. If a large organization like Walmart sees value in connecting to the local community and finding partners to accomplish a larger goal for measurable change, there is value in continuing to make progress and explore the resources. Large corporations are looking for ways to find partners to help them transform their organizations and their community relationships. The payoff for Walmart, or any corporation, is growing their customer loyalty. Lower prices are not enough for loyalty.

The connection to being part of the community and building a partnership to create a better community, one with better quality of life for the local residents, which includes employees, makes for a very compelling value proposition. This is where the new opportunities are for growth, but this is counterintuitive to many managers.

In a recent study of more than 400 corporations, government leaders and health professionals, East Texas Area Health Education Centers found taking action that delivered valuable results to be essential for a good corporate citizen. For employees and customers to work together with local businesses and leaders to inspire positive change is an immediate, focused goal for businesses. And when your partner is Walmart, which has the critical resources and commitment to act for change, results happen.

Kyle Spillers, a Market Manager at Walmart, put it best: "No one company or organization can do this alone. It will take us working together to make our communities healthier."

Rapid Action.

Rapid action is the essence of transformational growth. It is the telling sign of ideal partners. Transformational partners are ready for action and request that action happen soon. This is so often overlooked. It is a simple and vital new habit to start taking action on what is important to the potential partners. It builds momentum. Most clients wanting change place a high value on rapid communications. Our society is conditioned to want immediate response. Yet our resistance to change lets us put other issues into the top priorities instead of taking action toward a new outcome or goal.

When a partner wants to look at new ways to create a transition, there are three key points for working with partners to achieve it:

- Ask questions to define the roles of the people.

- Listen to the answers to find where both organizations involved meet to benefit the greater good of all.

- Respond with an approach, which is custom-made for the need as soon as possible and no later than a week after starting.

Each day you wait, you lose relevance and credibility at being a partner in a change effort.

Transitional partners are competing with over 1,000 emails a week, text messages, phone messages, Facebook posts, tweets, phone calls, and meetings. The faster you respond, the more prepared you are, the more people connect to you and want to work with you.

Our attention span is shorter by the day. It is less than a few seconds. When you meet with people who have a connection or interest in a partnership, the sooner you respond, the more likely it will work to the higher good of all.

What is the relevance in waiting?

So many times, fear of doing something wrong or looking silly keeps leaders from taking action to respond to opportunities. Also, mid-level managers are focusing on the next conference instead of the bigger picture and long-term goals. These goals are life-changing and results-driven. They represent the larger payoff, which changes the direction of companies and communities.

Start now.

For companies working in oil and gas, the consistent theme is to take action now and to have a sense of immediacy. One international oil executive said to me, "Where have you been? We are working on this now and want to do something right away." There is no resistance on why to change or debate on when to start. The answer is – now.

Another onshore energy production director said, "We are going to take action now and get something done right away." It is so refreshing and thrilling to work with people wanting to take action. This is important in change. Finding people who have a natural inclination to do something now makes change and transformation so much easier.

The basic point is to start.

Expense does not have to be an issue. Working with one executive director in heath care, we found the same focus and value in assessing a $250 activity and a $250,000 activity. This is understandable when you delve deeper into how important and inexpensive preventative health education and wellness motivation is for most organizations.

It is easy to avoid starting on larger, strategic efforts because they are not as urgent as an immediate activity. The more strategic $250,000 activity takes daily effort for a longer period of time. Longer-term activities do not provide a rush from a sense of completion.

Starting just 15 minutes of activity lets your mind process the actions. So many times while I have been writing during the past 10 years, something more urgent has come to the forefront of my to-do list. This means that writing, the activity, which is more strategic, does not get the attention and brainpower necessary for the optimum results.

Some wake up too late.

One health care director said, "Now I get it and I have resisted it for six months." "It" was the necessity of laying off one-third of her staff. The funding that was available for a smaller team is still there, just with other sources.

One foundation executive said, "Government entitlements will continue to shrink and the strongest organizations will have to find private funding." We have seen this happen.

So much pain can be avoided by taking action now.

It comes to you.

One very successful Texas criminal attorney, has a mantra, "Let it come to you." What we are talking about is a process.   Transformational

Partners provide a wake-up call that, while you are striving for a vision along the way, new abundance and partnerships come to you. New doors open which you do not expect. New ways of seeing situations, and new things which you do not plan on seeing, suddenly appear.

These new ways may not exactly be what you're looking for and many times this is better. When you have a vision, you have an objective from the partnership. During the conversation and when asking questions, if you are open, completely new things come your way: New creative projects, new business opportunities, new clients, and much better outcomes. The key is getting eye-to-eye with potential partners, stating your vision, and finding out what else opens up for you.

In a recent meeting with a large oil and gas company, a completely new possibility we had not considered in more than 10 years was discussed. It was an unexpected possibility that came from asking questions of and listening to partners. It will make a significant difference for many people. We could do it and, while it would not necessarily be easy, we will do it.

We had a previous conversation with a director at this company one year earlier and it did not have the same sense of urgency that there is today. He was new in the position then and now he has a renewed sense that something must be done.

Nature of Partners.

Partners are by nature transformational. Partners coming to work together on a project will alter how they do things to include others. Even in standard procedures, new discoveries can be made by altering the number of partners working together. Partners can lower costs and magnify revenues.

In energy, partners are required to go into new areas. Whether it is new geography or new technology as in green renewable energy, partners are required. No one person or company can manage the entire flow of energy from discovery to consumption on his or her own.

Each partner has a strength to bring to the dynamic relationship. Knowing how to ask the right questions, to listen to each partner's vision, and match the strengths together is essential for transformation to happen.

Finding 123 Main Street, Anywhere, USA.

After the research for opportunities and the Great Ideas Process™, it is vital to find local partners to work with agents of change leading the effort. These are the local people who are involved with foundations or industry leaders to improve the quality of life in a local community.

Working with one foundation, a health care client found a

partner willing to go to other foundation leaders to gain support for implementing the local plan for an area, which was an ideal 123 Main Street, Anywhere, USA. Taking action quickly with partners goes against many cultural norms in corporations. By the time some large clients get to do things, they are proven, tested, and effective. But are they still relevant?

Jim, a chemical engineer in a large petrochemical company said, "By the time our metrics and best practices are in sync with our competition, they have started something new. Comparing ourselves to others seems to bog us down and delay progress. The others are ignoring us and moving forward with a clear vision." Because we work with the other companies also, we see it too. Jim is right. Focusing on the new vision and learning how to change equips organizations, especially those in energy and health, to anticipate and see change coming. They are focused on their customers and consumers and need a larger focus. How are trends changing? What is next? What do we need to prepare for today so our organization can respond?

Those are some of the questions we begin to ask

when we are working with clients and their partners. Is it necessary to change to respond to changes you hope will not happen? Yes. We have found that a client such as East Texas Area Health Education Centers is on the cusp of implementing Making Our Communities Healthier, the initiative led by East Texas Area Health Education Centers.

In the private sector, a week is a lifetime. This is so different for so many health care providers to grasp in their thinking and culture. It requires a change of culture to respond to clients with a team, not a single person's success.

It is people working together, not just one person doing a star performance. If the star has jury duty or family issues, nothing happens. All progress stops.

There must be a way to continue. It is a team win and a team success.

Value of Transformational Partners.

In measuring the value of a transformational partner, start with three simple tests. Does this partner:

1. Commit to grow – Does the partner share your direction to grow, improve and continue to change?

2. Want the local community involved in their business – Does the partner want a role for their organization in making a larger impact in the community and world?

3. Care about the quality of life for the employees, customers, and the people they serve? Is the partner led by leaders who have a passion for the quality of

life for employees, customers, and the wider community?

Once you answer yes to at least two out of three of these simple points, you have a definite transformational partner, which working together with you can change the world, or at least your part of the world.

We see so many people who really want to partner and talk and so few that really take action together. Many times one person in the organization carries the fire to transformative change. It is important this person is like Joan of Arc or Mother Theresa, people who are for the positive outcomes of a movement and are ready to take action.

Fear Freeze.

Recognize that everyone is not a partner. The sooner organizations realize the difference between partners and contractors, the faster they are able to expand. The partnerships with people who don't want to be partners are in Fear Freeze. They are stopped at key points of conversion to the next level of success. One

example is a health care
organization that has two
internal leaders who decided
for 10 million other people not
to do the plan the leadership
and local partners developed
together. Literally, they are in
a fear freeze. Budget cuts are
coming and they would rather
lose their jobs and the jobs of
their colleagues than change.
The leadership of the
organization is struggling to
handle their personal
commitments and balance
them with the additional
attention needed to banish the
fear that has frozen the
organization.

Does One Person Really Make a Difference?

Yes. Again and again we see it. Melinda Sutherland of a large energy company said it best when she said, "You are sitting in a room and listening to the upcoming changes. You know that someone has to lead the transformation. Suddenly, you realize it is you. You are the one who can lead the change." She knows. Melinda led the transformational change for 55,000 people living in apartments who wanted to lower their utility costs and improve their quality of life by using natural gas appliances. Melinda led a team with four forward thinking marketing team members who decided to change.

Together they improved life for tens of thousands of people. That is transformational change.

VI. Conclusion

The Great Ideas Process™ is a step-by-step approach to creating revolutionary change. With each connection made, opportunities emerge to support sustainable increases of your targeted shared vision and specific plan goals. Within a developing partnership comes research on new trends in each respective industry. As such, new trends lead to new ventures, more people within the organization start to transform, special conferences are held, and conference papers are presented to capture the

essentials of these developments.

Through a continued focus on
the ever-changing market and
more opportunities to expand,
the global collaborations that
we facilitate mean profitability
for your organization. The
Great Ideas Process™ gives
your organization a framework
for growth.

Go to www.GreatIdeasCo.com for free information. For a complementary chat about a business situation or to schedule a speaking engagement, call 713.520.9600 or send an email to Jackie@greatideasco.com.

About the Author

Transformational Growth and Great Ideas Process™ is distilled wisdom from author, Jacqueline "Jackie" Broussard's two decades of cultivating imaginative ways with leaders, corporations, and communities to grow. Jackie's organic approach inspires positive change, richness and texture to empower clients locally and globally to create new partnerships that lead to growth, opportunity, and wealth. Her natural, simple approach encourages participants to navigate away from missed opportunities to Transformational Growth. Jackie presents, speaks, and trains around the world. Her Great Ideas Certification training provides leaders and external facilitators, consultants, and trainers with growth, opportunities, partnering, and communication tools. Jackie is an organic gardener, modern artist, teacher, volunteer, dog walker, dancer, and writer. She has a B.S. from Texas A&M in Psychology and MBA from the University of St. Thomas. For a complementary chat about your business situation, or a speaking engagement, call 713.520.9600 or Jackie@greatideasco.com.